THROUGH THE TREES

MARIA GILBERT

Through the Trees
Copyright © 2025 by Maria Gilbert.

All rights reserved. No part of this publication may be reproduced, distributed, or transmitted in any form or by any means, including photocopying, recording, or other electronic or mechanical methods, without the written consent of the publisher. The only exceptions are for brief quotations included in critical reviews and other noncommercial uses permitted by copyright law.

MILTON & HUGO L.L.C.
4407 Park Ave., Suite 5
Union City, NJ 07087, USA

Website: *www.miltonandhugo.com*
Hotline: *1- 888-778-0033*
Email: *info@miltonandhugo.com*

Ordering Information:
Quantity sales. Special discounts are granted to corporations, associations, and other organizations. For more information on these discounts, please reach out to the publisher using the contact information provided above.

Library of Congress Control Number:	2025920425
ISBN-13: 979-8-89285-705-5	[Paperback Edition]
979-8-89285-706-2	[Hardback Edition]
979-8-89285-707-9	[Digital Edition]

Rev. date: 11/21/2025

PART I

ROOTS
(Family and Silence)

I grew up in this house
Taught to keep my mouth shut
lower my voice
be quiet

Even when I think I'm fighting, I'm only stalling.

Because this house served its purpose.
But I'm too weak to end it
And I can't find it in me to leave it.

Eggshells

Life does not go well for me.
I'm the drama queen. I'm the one with too much attitude. Open up more.
You open up too much.
Tell me about yourself.
You talk too much.
You need to do better.
But you try too hard.

You're too mysterious; no one knows what you're thinking. You're lying.
I promise I won't be mad,
I can't believe you said that!
That's just not how it works.
I feel like you won't be honest with me if I asked.

Tell me the truth,
But love isn't enough.
Okay, if that's really what you want.
If you're sure, if you think so.
Who cares what you think?

Seventeen was stolen from me

Sex is sweet
But not at seventeen.

Within my family, I am an outsider.
Among friends, I am family.
During gatherings, I am present...but feel like a drifter.

Taken for Granted

As hard as I try
There is no moving forward where I am standing.

All that screams through my entire being is that this is a waste of my time trying to be a part of this family.

Run, run, *run*.

Some have always been right about our family—there's always something to talk about, to complain about.

My complaints feel valid, and I don't believe others complain because they want change. They bitch because they hold everyone else to high-cloud standards, everyone but themselves.

The Truth

After everything you made me do
Everything you put me through growing up

Feeling in denial.
That my family wouldn't believe me.
They wouldn't still love me.

I know that they chose me.
I told them about the abuse,
The lies
The hunting knife to my throat at nine.

How you'd kill me
You'd kill my dog
You'd cut my mother's throat in her sleep
If I ever told anyone.

Three years older than me
And yet you were the chemicals of all my night terrors

You were the eldest cousin
You were supposed to protect me

But instead, from ages five to thirteen I was your guide to what happens after Puberty

Or before really.

Is that why you went through so many Girlfriends?

Is it because you learned how to force them and throw them to the side?

All because I kept my mouth shut. I feel sorry for your dead parents.

There's a part of a story no one understands.
You all have a version of me inside your heads, but I'm exactly who I say I am.

I no longer do the unnecessary things that disturb my peace.
I no longer am willing to hide it all within.

Don't let my misfortunes in life make you worry. My mother gave me a wonderful childhood.
Her love overshadowed every stormy day.

PART II

STORM
(Addiction, Collapse, and Depression)

Exposed

The shadows are closing in. I welcome them as I embrace the storm taking over inside my head. The shadows are merely a man's cover as he crouches in the bushes waiting to attack from behind like a coward.

It is not the shadows who are at fault; it is man's for giving us something to be fearful towards in the first place.

The sun goes down, and the moon comes out. We know this; we still have the ability to choose. Be afraid or be cautiously at ease.

Bad things happen in the light.

Good things can happen in the dark.

Hollow

The waves crashing against the walls of my rib cage
The testimony of my inner self, that small voice
The voice that has grown into booming blood flow through my veins.

The same voice that echoes in jagged edges whenever the thought about being weighed down in life, one spot—crushes my train of thought. My entire wavelength of thinking.

Is the devil inside me? Or am I just ungrateful? Maybe a little gullible for believing it could ever be as great as the ending of my favorite literature.

How will I know if I'm with someone who very well may not be my soulmate beyond the grave?

Or above it.

July 31, 2021

334 days sober

To want something that's within reach.
It's as if I fought hard enough for something out of reach, and winning.
And, darling, you're a f——cking prize.
The best prize at the carnival.

And again, another drink—my soul is kept in a bottle on the reaper's shelf.
I'll never escape the pressure of the deformed man's impression of his peers. Never again will I tell the truth, especially to a man of an unsure mind.

Emotions don't mean a thing.
A grown man can't even think.

In progression
M. G.

I've let go of the steering wheel

Living out my predictions for where I'd eventually end up
Rock bottom, a shattered dream, a ripped shirt, and a cheap pair of blue jeans, torn at the hemming.

The paper with my last testament jammed deep in my larynx
The flow of air shutting down as my panic thickens.

Eyes stinging, all efforts lost as the left side of my jacket drips with blood that has escaped my sleeve.

It can't wait, I believe is what I said as my conscience attempted to pull me out of the cycle I allowed myself to wander aimlessly in every chance I felt was deserving.

"When will you believe me?"

The answer is, how long would it take for her to stop believing in him?

The cycle carries on, and for once, as the years went on,
It is she who has the tables turned, her credibility washing down the storm drain.

And so it ends, while my demise slowly begins.

M. G.

...heartbreak, alcoholism, no boundaries between living and dying

Insomnia

I keep telling myself that I'll start living for myself and not anyone else, but it still seems like that's all I'm doing. I keep getting pulled back in. I just care too much about others, and I lose myself doing so. *I'm just tired. I'm sure I look that way to others. I'm tired of being manipulated into helping others, and I'm tired of certain people making promises and then not keeping them.*
I'm tired of never having enough money because I'm always helping someone and feeling obligated to do so.
I just want this to be my year.

I have really bad depression and anxiety.
This has caused me to have medical problems, and it's made it hard to get out of bed or leave the house on time for anything.
I feel empty. Not suicidal at all, nothing like that.
Just numb, and every time I start feeling again, something or someone makes me creep back inside of myself.

I'm just *tired of being strong all the time, and I'm tired of being tired.*
Tired of trying so hard for other people when the cycle never stops.

If I don't stop helping, I'll never be able to move forward, building a life and future for myself, for us. It's a team effort, but *I'm the only one, it feels, that's on my team.*

This is my cycle of guilt for others and betrayal towards myself.

Sometimes, I just wish that I could put a bullet in my mouth because I can't live with myself anymore.

There are times that I don't know how to keep going because people don't trust me, and I don't know how to show them that they can because I too have made mistakes when it comes to those who I want to have trust in me.

You can't explain to someone what it means to be depressed.

Only what it means to feel the weight of the heaviest dumbbell on your collarbone while the rest of your body is floating, as if there's no gravity in the solar system.

Manic

When the only thing keeping you alive is the anger that makes you thrive

And the love you must attend to someone because they mean more than death to you... But what happens when that love means no harm, but a helpful ear, stern advice?

Suddenly, you feel as if you should have never existed to know that you caused them pain, by having gone too far

When you should have known when to stop yourself.

Your ego taking over, your anger going too far

Turning into a madness of sadness and

Anxietal stress that you can't process or confess yourself to.

Because then your ego loses.

As it should.

There's so much inner agony towards my pitiful life.

If someone told me that I've died and this is hell, I'd believe them.
I'm a starving artist bound by noes and opinions.
I've got so much inspiration and no authority to display it.

My hands are tied.
Every day is mediocre, and I am isolated revolving around three people repeatedly. I can't allow them to steal my light and my life.

All My Friends

We're not civilians
But we're people.
So what if our problems, you know...
The reasons we end it.
What if it's because both worlds cling together
and stopping our heartbeats is
the only form of silence we receive?

One last bang is the eye of our storm
Calm and peaceful at last.

Maybe that's why I lost so many brothers and sisters.

Don't you just love the sweet tears and cold sweats of nightmares? Even earning myself a racing heart as the panic begins to fade, the whooshing running through my veins and into my ears.

They say to watch something lighthearted before you fall asleep.

I guess it doesn't always work.

Anyway, there's step 4 for you. Here's my inventory for what I've been pent up on since my dog got snipped and my wrist snapped. I'm stuck in my childhood home.

Where I slept and cried and felt completely unworthy as a teenager and the one that made me wish I could be numb forever, so to believe that I am still sober to this day

Well I guess it's a blessing because all of my depression and anxiety and regret after my rape at the ripe age of seventeen is flooding back, and I can't stop thinking about all the bad I've caused and hardships I've created because I had resentments.

I will never do this again.
I will never trust someone when they say they'll do something, not until they are taking action in that direction.

Not until they've done it.
I will no longer be the one people come to.

I will no longer be used.

I am no more than a me pleaser
Satisfaction is for me and myself alone.

Anxiety is a steel grip on my lungs
Smothering me from within.

Forcing me to my knees.
Struggling to breathe.

I haven't breathed for three damn weeks. This has taken so much out of me.

Wheezing on the exhale
Aspiration on my tongue.

Medication isn't a worthy fix
But this book is.

Part III

FAITH
(Searching, Questioning, Glimpses of Light)

Rewind

If there is a *God*, does he have a floppy
A drooling, an adorning tongue?
Will he ever disrespect me, like the men at the tavern would...?
His teeth bearing, lip snarling
Tail in between his ego—oh, the way those men try to seduce you.

Can I live eternity forgotten to a partner with two legs?
And so, I kick myself, once again.
Have faith that *He* is better than any man.

In Blue

If there is a day where the light is gray
I'll think of you
Where I won't be blue

Living a life that's full is a lot harder when you don't believe you deserve to. Eventually, life will give you the sucker punch that you need to convince you otherwise.

If not for me, then for whom?
Who else is looking out for me?
Who else besides God himself?

Why do all expectations land on me?

It's funny
Because I'm pretty sure that dogs have all the answers.

How else can you explain it?
You're going to have to write it out into a poem for me.

"It's always, 'Get some rest.'

"It's never, 'Take time for yourself because you have to help everyone else.'"

Look at all those leaves
Shaking in the breeze
Not afraid of falling off.

Every day, I think of how the sky is much closer with you up there and me down here.

Fighting for medicine.
Fighting for appointments.
Fighting for everything.
But fighting to be taken seriously...
Bullshit.

Aging is a bizarre concept.
Hard to comprehend
2017 Okinawa to me is,
...
Boiled peanuts,
Head scratches,
Hazel green eyes looking up at me.
The smell of cigarettes and a hard day's work.
And a ladybug tattoo.

My Confession

There have been moments where just like everyone else, I am fooled.

And like a plague, there it is
The burden of remembering.

They're all like sheep...unaware that amongst them is a wolf in hiding.
Trying to blend in with the rest of them.

Making them smile.
Making them laugh.

I used to wish that I could be one of them.

But my curse is to keep an eye on him. To make sure he remembers what he did.

Whom he did it to.
And that it never happens again.

I am your Grim Reaper
Awaiting your mistakes.
Your slipup.

And I'll take that responsibility to my grave.

Part IV

SURVIVAL
(Defiance, Healing, and Renewal)

The Fighter

The fighter comes and goes; it comes in tidal waves.

When you learn how strong you really are—and by learn, I mean you experience it in different ways—you realize the time and place appropriate on when to give in and deal or to survive the situation you're in and walk away, leaving flames.

That's what you are

A flame that never stops burning.

You are thriving when you're strong, and

You are brilliant when you're vulnerable.

Let yourself be vulnerable for the right people and the right reasons. You'll know when to be strong and how strong to be.

Your gut is your best decision maker.

Your heart is how you show your soul to the world.

And your brain is what you use to write things down to make your thoughts look pretty

M. G

Survivor

So I've been thinking about it.

He asked me last week when I was trying to tell him how I was feeling. "Why do you do that? Why do you make yourself seem like a victim?" I haven't seen him since. I haven't spoken to him since, and I realize today that I don't want to.

That's all he sees me as.

I'm not a f——ing victim. I'm a f——ing survivor, and he can shove his head and his nasty words up his ass.

For once, I'm not going to be the one who apologizes.

I'm damaged, and when I need to be alone, you have to leave me for a short time so I can find a way to get back on my feet again. You have to let me go a few days without showering or without leaving my room because that's just the kind of person that I am. The burdens that I carry can never compare to the words I give in explanation.

Move onto me in a different universe

One far enough away from me here

As I'm finally living in this one.

Wings of Freedom

A calm overcomes my mind where the
Billowing quakes used to roar
Anxiety used to take over
Now, it's at a hum.

I wonder how I got here
Look how far I've come.

An overwhelming journey
A path to grace
A sound mind.

Fierce

I had to choose to love myself.

I had two options...

Keep doing what I was doing to very well
End up like my aunt and sweet cousin

Or I could love myself fiercely.

For eight weeks, I put all my focus into
Finding the love for myself and how to heal
The bleeding wound that led me to drink...
And I think it made all the difference.

I had a spiritual awakening.

Billow

If my body showed up in the water, I
Couldn't say I was surprised of it
Happening in such a way. Because
Drowning would be such a peaceful way to
Die. The waves just taking you under, you
Let them. They take you further; you let the
Streams of bubbles pass you by, and you die. You just die, peacefully.

Dylan Gossett

Fuck dreaming
I might just stop breathing.

One sister
One niece
Almost a daughter
Breaking that booze infested cycle...

It wasn't just for me.
Congratulations to me on five years sober,
Rather than an expiration date on a gravestone.

I often wonder if my dog knows how often he's saved me.

I wonder if he feels my gratitude every morning I wake up and get to look at him.

I believe everything that I survived
It was meant to prepare me for the strength it takes to break through the jaded film I barricaded myself behind.
To be great.
To be successful.

Don't you dare convince me,
Who has never asked for anything,
Who has never complained to you,
Who was willing to show you the love the Universe rests in the palms of my touch,
The love God wishes me to spread,
That you'll be there for me if I ever reach out.

Don't you dare let me trust you,
Because you weren't.

There's a sadness within her.
One that consumes her.
Intoxicating her entire existence.

(6-9-24; 2:19 a.m.)

I was doing all right.

Letting the breeze hit me
As I roll down the truck windows my arm flowing freely out the window.

I openly let the sun caress my cheeks, bringing a smile upon my lips.

And then I was brought back to before.
When I didn't know that it was all a big fat lie.

And that's all it took to falter my reinvented peace.
My facade.
The security blanket I wrapped myself in.

Now I'm embracing the darkness
Deciding if I should save myself
Or let my light be snuffed out.

Being too stubborn to give up
I'll likely just turn the music up
Pretending to myself to pretend to everyone else.

M. G.

A Quote from My Mom

Mom: "Stay positive. Remember, you always end up on top."

And I did, every time. This book being published
Is proof that every impossible
Day that I endured, I survived to live another.

Releasing my trapped words to the public
Is so therapeutic. It is validation and it has
Allowed me to freely feel the emotions that
Come with the title of a "published author."
A tight billow has soared within me.

As of late

- I have found the strength within myself to set boundaries with the people that have proven difficult to get along with.
- I have become the savior that the younger version of me would look up to.
- I have broken the chaotic alcoholic cycle that many in my family have endured for generations and being the only one so far to do so successfully for five years running.
- I pray every day to my God who loves me, and I know this wouldn't be possible without His blessings.
- I have healed myself, along with the help of several therapists through the VA's powerful PTSD clinic in Ann Arbor, Michigan.

All this to shape my own path of resilience to pursue my dream of being at peace with myself and my past.

I appreciate everyone who believed me when I told them what he did to me. You are the reason this book finally came to light. Thank you for helping me find my voice so I can push it to reach others that may need one too.

I want to thank my mom for teaching me the resilience and inner strength that it took to survive my time in the Marines. Without your words of wisdom, I would have strayed down a one-way path long ago.

I would like to send a prayer of gratitude towards my dear friend, Joanne. She was always graceful, even up to her last breath. Thank you for always having faith in me and showing such interest in my hobbies. I think of you as this book gets published, your warm smile and gentle eyes. May you rest heavenly in peace.

Through the Trees

My opinion? God talks to me through the trees when I'm alone in the morning.
Then when I've strayed too far from my path, my spirit awakens my unconscious mind of conversations that don't exist.

Everyone else? I'm nuts.

"So that's why you message me?"

You're the conversations that don't exist.